Digital Mastery for Women

The First 5 Digital Marketing Components You Need to Master in Your Business

By Vanessa Collins, CDMP

Heart Thoughts Publishing
Floyds Knobs, IN

Printed in the United States of America

ISBN-13: 978-1546597643
ISBN-10: 1546597646

First Printing, 2017

Heart Thoughts Publishing
P.O. Box 536
Floyds Knobs, IN 47119
www.HeartThoughtsPublishing.com
Vanessa@HeartThoughtsPublishing.com

Thank You...

for purchasing this book. As my gift to you, please visit www.VanessaCollinsLLC.com/DMFWBook to get access to our FREE Online Resource Page that has exclusive videos training, worksheets and other resources designed specifically for this book.

Also, don't forget to leave a review on Amazon.

Dedication

To all the women entrepreneurs that are making it happen every day. I honor you!

Table of Contents

Introduction

Mastering digital technology can be a challenge for many women entrepreneurs, especially since for many women, we have bought into the idea that technology is a "man's world." Man's world or not, technology is something that we, as women, will need to embrace if we are going to experience growth in our businesses. The key to accomplishing this is to understand what technology you need in your business and determining the best strategy for you to implement it. Do you have time but you are short on funds? You may need to spend that time to learn how to implement some of the basic things in your business until you can hire someone to do it. Are you short on time because of your job or family commitments? If so, you may need to spend some money to hire a team to help you. In either case, you need to understand the types of systems you need to have in place.

Overview of the Relationship Based Marketing Methodology

Before we talk systems, we must understand the basics of marketing relationships. Marketing relationships follow the same rules as human relationships because at the end of the day, businesses don't buy from businesses. It is people in business who buy from other people in business.

You need to use your digital marketing power to cultivate relationships with people. Just as in human relationships, you can move too fast in social media relationships. You would find it awkward and weird for someone to ask you to go away with them for a week's vacation to foreign place on a first date. Even if you really wanted a vacation and had told your friends about how you wanted to visit a certain destination, you would be leery about going away with someone you just met.

Why? It isn't the offer. You love vacations, you love to travel, you have always wanted to go to that destination. It's not the offer, it's where you are in relationship with the person that is making the offer. I can have the best products and services in the world and they could be the exact products and services you need, but if I don't take time to cultivate a relationship with you, you will not buy my services.

This is why a lot of people claim that social media does not work in terms of making sales for your business. They may get some likes and a few comments but they have not experienced major success using social media. The reason they are not successful is not because social media doesn't work. Let me be clear, social media works. Over 80% of my paid business comes from social media. I have authors that I have published that I have NEVER met except through Facebook and they have paid me hundreds and thousands of dollars. I landed 2 of my biggest clients using social media and they paid me 4 and 5 figures before I ever met them. Social media works, you just need to know how to work it.

However, great relationships and good vibrations are not enough to build a truly successful business. You need to have a few systems in place. In this book, we will cover the first 5 systems that you need to master in your business. These are:

- Your Sales Funnel
- Your Content
- Your Paid Traffic
- Your Social Media
- Your Email Marketing

Let's look at each of these.

Your Sales Funnel

Your sales funnel is the blueprint for your customer's journey. How does your audience go from being a curious spectator to a paid customer and then to a raving fan and brand ambassador? It is through having a relationship with you and your brand.

Your Content

As an entrepreneur, the more that you accept the responsible of educating your audience about the industry or issues that they are concerned about, the more they will see you as an expert and the more they will rely on you for the answers to their problems. Content Marketing allows you to use your content to do just that. This content is not the same content that you are selling as your products and services but it should be based on it.

Your Paid Traffic

Many entrepreneurs complain that they can't get traffic to their websites. It is very easy to get traffic to your site. You pay for it, plain and simple. I hate to be the bearer of bad news but if you are just starting out, I don't care how much search engine optimization (SEO) that you use, it is going to be extremely difficult for you to get the organic traffic that you need to sustain your business. You are a business and you must advertise just like every other business.

Your Social Media

Building your tribe is a crucial part of your marketing plan. Social media can help you do this very easily. But, how do you get social media to work for you? To be most successful on social media, you need to have a strategy in place.

Your Email Marketing

Email marketing is not dead. It is very much alive. Having followers on Facebook, Periscope and Twitter is wonderful but you must get those people on your list. If these third-party platforms close your account, you have lost those contacts. The old saying, "The money is in the list," is true. The problem is that most entrepreneurs think that you only use your email list to promote your products and services. That can't be further from the truth. You use email marketing to engage your audience and nurture the relationship.

Chapter 1 – The Bottom line of business

Before we start to navigate the waters of digital marketing, we need to remember why we are here. Why do you even want to get into these waters? The answer is obvious, you want to get out here to grow your business. So, let's quickly talk about the bottom line of business.

The bottom line of business is very simple. You must get your products and services into the hands of your customers. In exchange for your products and services, your customers will give you some sort of compensation. That may be in the form of money, endorsements or even their e-mail address. All three of these are important.

How do you get your products and services into the hands of your customers? There are 5 critical things that you need to do to make this happen. Everything you do in business must support at least one of these objectives.

You must:

- Find your customers or make it easy for them to find you.

- Find out what your customers need.

- Inform, educate and convince your customers that you can meet their needs.

- Deliver your product/service in way that suits your customer.

- Have systems in place to receive compensation. That compensation may be in the form of currency or an email address.

Don't Play Hide and Seek - Let Customers Find You

Just as it is important for your customers to be able to find your physical location if you have a brick and mortar operation, it is important that they can find you online. Although this may seem like a "no brainer," you may be surprised how many business owners miss this. Perhaps you are not surprised. Maybe you have had the experience of wanting to find a particular business but couldn't because you didn't remember the exact name or website address. You searched under something that you thought would be close, but, you couldn't find them. So, you ended up going with another business. Your digital marketing strategy must include helping your clients find you.

Website – Your Main Cyber Real Estate

Your website is your key piece of real estate in cyberspace. This is where the magic happens. This is your home. This is where you want to invite your customers to come, interact and learn how you can help them with their problem. Unlike our physical homes, which is about our likes and preferences, your website should be about your customer. It should be inviting and easy to navigate. The goal should be giving the customers what they need.

Make sure that your site is search engine optimized (SEO). Although Google and other search engines seem to change their search algorithms on a regular basis, there are still some best practices that never get old. Make sure that your domain name reflects your service, product or brand as much as possible. Avoid using "cute" names unless it is part of your brand or product name.

I remember my first website which was geared towards moms making extra money on the internet. I thought momXtracash.com would be a cute name.

However, I quickly found that not many people search on how to make "xtra" cash on the internet.

In addition to having a domain name that reflects your products and brand, try to get a domain name that reflects your actual name. This domain name can be for a simple, one page website that directs people to all your other websites. People may forget your brand or product name; however, if you left a good impression with them, they may remember your actual name.

There are tons of good, free information about SEO and how to make sure that people can find your site. Take the time to do the research and get this step right.

Social Media

Regardless to what you think about social media, you must get in the game to really grow your business. While having a website is extremely important, people are not typically hanging out on your website. People will come to your site to get what they need and then they will leave. Since most websites are not designed in such a way as to encourage dialogue or interaction, you need to go where the people are. People are hanging out on social media. They are posting their information on Facebook, their pictures on Instagram, their random thoughts on Twitter and their questions in LinkedIn groups. We will discuss more details about your social media strategy in a later chapter.

At the time of this writing (April 2017), these are the top 5 social media platforms according to ebizmba.com. Do you have a presence on these?

- Facebook - 1.5 Billion Estimated Unique Monthly Visitors

- YouTube - 1.499 Billion Estimated Unique Monthly Visitors

- Twitter - 400 Million Estimated Unique Monthly Visitors

- Instagram – 275 Million Estimated Unique Monthly Visitors

- LinkedIn – 250 Million Estimated Unique Monthly Visitors

These social media sites are phenomenal tools for finding customers and being found by customers. With over a billion unique monthly visitors, they have become a hub for all things social. This means that they have become a hub for all things business because many people conduct business is a "social way." This is nothing new. Back in the day, many deals where brokered on golf courses and in country clubs. Today it is Facebook fan pages, Messenger and

LinkedIn connections that people are using to expand their sales and networks.

Make sure that your social media presence represents the best side of you. Although it may be tempting to air your dirty laundry and lash out about people and issues, consider how this will look to your customers. Remember, what you share on Facebook and any other social media can be shared or captured (via screen shot) and disseminated to the world.

It's Really Not About You – Find Out What Your Customers Need

This is a cornerstone of business philosophy that many have forgotten. We often try to put the proverbial cart before the horse on this one. We may feel inspired to develop a great product or service that will solve a big problem or answer a troubling question for someone. After we do the work of putting everything together, we present the world our great product. We position our product on social media or flood the inboxes of our email subscribers with invitations to purchase our latest and greatest program. Then we discover a new problem; no one is jumping to buy.

We may have solved a great problem and answered a huge question but we must find the people who have that great problem or need an answer to that huge question. We often solve problems that our market doesn't see as a problem. We are answering questions that no one is asking.

We must find out what our customers need. What are the problems they are actually having? What questions are they actually asking? We will cover this in more detail in our chapter on Social Media.

Help Me Help You - Inform, Educate and Convince

Once you know who your customers are and what they need, you must inform, educate and convince them that you can meet their needs. Let's look at each of these separately.

Inform

You must inform your customers that you can meet their needs. While this may seem easy enough, many of us fail to do this. How many times has someone said to you, "I didn't know that you offered that service," or "I didn't know that you had that type of product"? You must find a way to get the message to your customers about how you can help solve their problems.

Here are a few simple things you can do.

- **Make sure that your social media profiles are complete and comprehensive.** Some social media profiles like LinkedIn rank very high in search results. Make sure that your profile contains the keywords that your customers are searching on.

- **For keyword research, use a tool like Google Planner, formerly known as Google Keyword Tool.** Although this tool is part of the Google Adwords site, you do not need to purchase an Adword campaign in order to use the tool.

- **Make sure that you update your website often with your latest products and services.**

Schedule a time once a quarter to review your social media profiles and websites.

Educate

Sometimes you will find that you need to educate your customers on what they need. They may understand the problem they are having but not know what solutions are available to them. This is a case of "not knowing" what you don't know.

One of the most effective ways to educate your customers is to offer great, free content that will address their problems. Why free? Many people will not value a solution when they are not aware of the problem. For instance, suppose you have developed a great product to help people optimize their marketing funnels. Depending on who your customers are, many may not even know what a "marketing funnel" is. Therefore, they will not see the value of your product.

However, if you did a free webinar on how to improve sales using an optimized marketing funnel, you have a better chance of increasing your own sales. This process allows you to address a problem that your customer understands very well (the need to improve sales) with a solution that they may not be very familiar with (optimized marketing funnels).

Convince

Once you have informed your customers of what you can do for them and possibly even educated your customers on a particular product/service, you must convince them that you are the one they should choose. It's a simple question. Why should they hire you? Why should they buy your product?

There is a ton of literature out there about the psychological reasons people purchase the way that they do. Consider some of these reasons.

- **Proven Track Record** – People may buy from you because you have proven that you can deliver the results that you claim. Make sure that you have a system in place for asking and receiving testimonials from previous clients. Post those on your website and other social media platforms.

- **Brand Recognition** – People may buy from you because they recognize you as a leader in the industry. Becoming a leader in an industry does not mean that you must be number 1 or even number 100. It means that you are active in the industry that you have chosen. That could mean attending the right networking functions or being part of the right online communities.

- **Gut Feeling** – People may buy from you because they feel something when they visit your website or see your social media post. Don't underestimate the power of "gut feelings." While it may seem like there is little that you can do to influence this, that is not true. Everything that you do sets a tone that others see and feel. What tone does your website present? Is it happy and uplifting or is it strong and powerful? This is where knowing your customer is key. A fitness website that has a strong and powerful tone may not appeal to someone that is looking to gradually get into exercise. However, it may be the exact tone needed to attract someone interested in bodybuilding.

Have It Your Way – Deliver Products and Services the Way Your Customer Wants Them

I grew up during the time where there were encyclopedia salespeople. These people would go door to door selling sets of these wonderful books. If you could afford a set of encyclopedias, which could cost several hundreds of dollars, your family was doing well, especially where I lived.

Then a funny thing happened. Personal computers were born. As personal computers advanced, the type of data they could display advanced. I remember getting my first CD that contained the entire encyclopedia on it. I stared at the disc in amazement. If an encyclopedia salesman had knocked on my door at that very moment, they would have been very unhappy.

Are you delivering your products and services in a way that best suits your customers? If not, you are leaving money on the table. Remember the bottom line of any business. You must get your products and services into the hands of your customer. This is the step where many complaints arise and repeat business and referral customers are lost. You must understand the delivery preferences of the customers and how to compensate when something goes wrong.

In this technology age, many people prefer content delivered in a digital format. You must make sure to include this in your offerings. For instance, if you are an author, you should consider having your book available not only in print form but also in eBook and audio book format, especially if that is the way your customer prefers the content. You will notice that many top selling business books are available in eBook and audio book formats because many business executives like to listen to content on their tablets and smartphones. Here, again, it is important to know your customer. Do your customers like to get your type of information in digital format? If so, make sure you can deliver it that way.

Show Me the Money - Receiving Compensation

One would think that having systems in place to receive compensation would be the easiest thing in the world. But it isn't and you know this from experience.

Have you ever attempted to make purchase all to find out that the business does not accept the type of currency that you have available to you at that moment? It is frustrating and, unfortunately, it is the death of many sales. Remember, we must not only be able to deliver the product/service into our customer's hands, we must be able to receive some type of compensation for it.

Old Money/New Money, Green Money/Blue Money

In the good old days, cash was king. Although credit cards were accepted in most places, your cash was always welcome. That is what I like to refer to as the new "old money." However, in the new era of online shopping, your cash is not very useful. If you want to make a purchase on Amazon or another online store, you must be able to pay with something other than cash.

I refer to the "other" type of currency as "blue money." When we think of the color of money, we typically think green because paper money was green (I am not quite sure what color it is now). However, the icons for most online currency systems seem to all have the color blue in them (Look at the icons for PayPal, Chase Bank or PNC Bank). Not only must you have access to some type of online banking service ("blue" money) to purchase on the internet, you must be able to accept "blue" money from your customers.

At a minimum, you must have a system like PayPal or something similar to accept payments from customers. You must be able to securely accept credit cards payments. There are many shopping cart services that will allow you to offer convenient and safe payment processing for your customers. Do your homework.

Other Forms of "Payment"

But remember, currency is not the only compensation that you need. Sometimes you need to expand your mailing list and generate leads. You may do this with what is known as a "lead magnet." We will discuss lead magnets more in another chapter. However, to offer a lead magnet, you need to have a system in place to accept their email address. You need an autoresponder in place to deliver the content once they sign up for it.

Each of the aspects of digital marketing that we will discuss in this book is designed to support one or more of the areas we just discussed. If you are doing activities that do not support the bottom line of your business, you are wasting value time.

Chapter 2 – Your Products and Services

Now that you understand your bottom line, it's time to talk products and services. All the digital marketing stuff we will discuss in the upcoming chapters is only good if you have some products and services that you are offering.

Deciding your product line must start with your target audience. This is where many entrepreneurs struggle. We develop products and services and then we must go out and try to find the people who want those products and services. Although it is not an impossible task, it can be difficult. There is an easier way to do this.

Instead of starting with the product, let's start with the target audience. Consider these 3 questions.

- Who do YOU want to work with?
- What problem do THEY have?
- How can you monetize the solution?

Your Ideal Client

Here is the great thing about entrepreneurship. You get to work with the people you want to work with. Do you want to work with women business owners? Great. You want to work with single moms? Awesome. You want to work with aspiring writers? Fantastic. Find out what problems they have that you can solve.

The Client's Pain Point

I know this is starting to sound like a broken record. You must know and understand your client's pain point. What problems do they have? What problems do they think they have? Your customers may think they have a revenue generation problem when in actuality they have a system automation problem. If your specialty is system automation, you can develop products that will help them increase their revenue through system automation. How you package your solution should be determined by your client's pain point. It they are looking for a revenue generation solution, that's how you package it. If they are looking for a system automation solution, that's how you package it. It's the same product, just packaged differently.

Monetize the Solution

Now we are ready to get the camera rolling, the keyboard cracking and the microphone going. It's time to develop some products and services that offer solutions for your client's problems. One of my mentors, Che Brown, always says, "People will pay you TODAY for a problem that you solve for them TODAY." If it is a big enough problem, people will pay for the solution.

There are many ways that you can monetize your message or the solutions that you provide. I recently did a video series on 12 Ways to Monetize Your Message. I have included access to this on the Online Resource Page found at www.VanessaCollinsLLC.com/DMFWBook.

Here are the 12 ways I use to monetize my message.

1. Books
2. eBooks
3. Audio Books
4. Webinars
5. Online Courses
6. Teleseminars
7. Speaking
8. Certification Programs
9. Membership Programs
10. Special Reports

11. Coaching
12. Mobile Apps

Your Product Line

You can develop your product line by choosing several items from the list above. Every product line can have different components and it is based on your market and how your target audience likes to receive content.

I personally believe that every product line should have a book. All publishing biases aside (well, most of them aside), I can't think of any business that would not benefit from having a book. A book is a great way to inform and educate your audience and it is a great way to establish yourself as an expert. Of course, once you have the book, you have the content for the eBook and the audio book. You kill 3 birds with one stone.

Webinars, teleseminars and special reports can be used to promote your other products such as classes, coaching and membership programs. Online courses are great because they allow you to share your content with many people at one time. Membership programs are one of my favorite offerings because it is a source of recurring revenue. Speaking opportunities are always great because you can share your message live and generate interest for other products you have. Think about your message, the problems you solve and the people you solve those problems for and then develop your product line.

Now that we understand the bottom line of business and we have our products and services in place, the fun begins. Let's get these great solutions into the hands of our target market.

Chapter 3 - Understand Your Sales Funnel

What makes a good date? Is it the magnificent restaurant, the stimulating conversation or the surprise gift you received at the beginning of the evening? Is it any ONE thing or is it the experience as a whole?

In my opinion, the whole idea of "marketing" is taking your prospective client on a series of fantastic dates, with each date designed to strengthen the relationship. As with human relationships, the goal is not to just get to one moment in time, i.e. to the altar. The goal is to "grow old together."

Your sales funnel is a set of sequences designed to do just that. The purpose is to move the relationship forward. It is about giving your clients one great experience with you after another. You may start out solving a small problem for your client with a low-cost product. The goal is to progress so that you are solving more complex problems for your client with higher priced solutions.

Typically, your sales funnel will have the following components:

- Ungated Information
- Lead Magnet
- Tripwire Offer
- Core Offer
- Upsell Offer
- Downsell Offer

Let's look at each of these.

Ungated Information

Scenario 1: Imagine you are at function and you catch the eye of someone that is interested in meeting you. They come over to you, introduce themselves to you and you begin chatting. You may talk about why you are at the function or something related to the function that you both have in common. After chatting it up for 30 minutes, you realize that this is really a nice person and you wouldn't mind seeing them again. At the end of the conversation, you exchange cards and make a promise to keep in touch or even meet for coffee in a few days.

That sounds like the beginning of a great relationship. Even if you just remain friends, things have started on a good note. You are probably more likely to respond to their text messages or phone calls the next day because the evening didn't go like this...

Scenario 2: Imagine you are at function and you catch the eye of someone that is interested in meeting you. They come over to you, introduce themselves to you and you begin chatting. Immediately they begin to try to sell you on their product, service or themselves. They tell you that you are crazy if you talk to anyone else at the gathering because they have everything you will ever need. But, you better act fast if you want to take advantage of this great opportunity. For you to demonstrate that you are worthy of this opportunity, you need to have some "skin in the game." They are convinced that if you let them, they can grow your business, expand your products or be the love of your life. But you must act now. So, they ask you to invest in yourself by purchasing their $997 product or going somewhere with them that is a little more "private."

Most likely, you will not have to ignore this person's texts or calls because you probably didn't give them your information anyway. You got far, far away from this person as soon as you could.

Why was scenario 1 better for relationship building? You were able to get to know the person first before you committed to moving to the next level. Although the "next level" only consisted of giving your contact information, that is a big next step for entrepreneurs.

As entrepreneurs, we hate unproductive contact. That includes unwanted emails, social media messages and text messages. Admit it, you have screened your calls before. You have glanced at your Messenger before and decided NOT to click it because you didn't want the person to know you had seen their message. People must earn the right to get our attention.

That is exactly what ungated information does for you as a business owner. It helps you earn the right to get the attention of your audience. This is information that people can get that requires no commitment on their part. You are demonstrating your knowledge about the topic and how that knowledge can help them. This information should not require any information for them to access it. Although this information is free it must be GOOD. If you waste people's time, they will not give you their money.

Examples of ungated information include:

- Blog posts on your site
- Blog posts on LinkedIn
- Livestream
  - Periscope
  - Facebook Live

If your ungated information is good, people will want to move forward in the relationship. However, you must have something for them to move forward to.

Lead Magnet

Now it's time to get some information. Remember scenario 1? If you enjoyed the conversation with that person, in order to have another conversation, you will have to give up some information. If you are going to "keep in touch" you must provide information for that to happen.

In your marketing, this is done with what is known as a lead magnet or freemium. This is free, quality content that solves 1 problem in exchange for an email address. In addition to developing content that can be used as a lead magnet (we will cover that in a later chapter), you must have a way to capture the email address and deliver the content.

This is where you begin the gift giving part of the relationship. But the gift cannot be random. The lead magnet should lead to your tripwire and core product. Also, make sure that the lead magnet is appropriate for where your customer is in their journey with you. When first meeting someone, inviting them to coffee to continue a great conversation is great. Inviting them to go away with you for the weekend to continue the conversation is a little creepy.

Similarly, in business, your lead magnet must match where you are in the relationship. We will talk more about this later.

Tripwire

Now the fun begins. It is time to get a commitment. This is the point where you make an offer for your potential customer to become a real customer. It's time for them to pull out their credit card.

Your tripwire offer should be a low priced, high value item. Depending on your market, it should be priced under $20 ($7 has tested to be the optimal price). It should have a valued of $49 to about $200.

There are many in the digital marketing community that swear by the use of tripwire offers. There are others that are dead set against them.

What's the answer? You should try it for yourself and your market. I have seen a lot of success with them.

Examples of tripwire offers include:

- Workshop or Class
- One module of a multi module series
- Evergreen audio or video recordings

Core Offer

Your entire funnel should be driven by your core offer. What you offer as a lead magnet and tripwire should lead to the purchase of your main product. Since you may have many products in your business, you may have many sales funnels.

What is your core offer? I know this sounds like an easy question and if you can answer it you are ahead of the game. Many entrepreneurs have many products but they have not organized then in such a way that there is a progression from one product to another. Many times, the way to increase revenue in our business is not to find more clients but to sell more products and services to the clients we have.

The price of your main offer depends on your industry. Keep in mind that your core offer is often not your high-priced offer. Keep that for the upsell offer.

Examples of core offers include:

- Monthly membership - $25 - $149
- One time purchase - $49 - $499
- Group Coaching - $150 - $997

This is often a "do it yourself" or "done with you" solution. Also, this product offers limited access to you. The more of your time that is involved in delivering the solution, the higher the price.

Upsell

This is a more extensive version of your core product and is often the "done for you" solution to your core product. It may be addons that your core product doesn't offer.

We have seen upsells used in marketing often but we may not have been aware of it. When you buy a new car, there are features that come standard (that's the core offer). If you want to get additional features, you must upgrade (that's the upsell).

Upsell offers can range from $997 to $20K or $30K. Don't let those numbers scare you. Many entrepreneurs have a $20K - $25K package that offers a complete solution for their clients. If you don't have a $25K package, you should.

Downsell

Sometimes your upsell package is more than what your client needs. You can offer what is known as a downsell offer which is a lower priced option of your upsell package. This package doesn't offer as much as the upsell but it is still higher priced than the core product. Please note, **this is NOT your Upsell product ON sale.**

Pulling it all together

Go through your product offerings and determine your tripwire, core offers, upsell and downsell offers. Develop any content (blog post, livestream broadcasts or lead magnets) that you need to get people introduced to your product line. See the examples on the Online Resource Page for example sales funnels I have in my business.

www.VanessaCollinsLLC.com/DMFWBook

Chapter 4 - Your Content

Now that you have your inventory of products and services organized, it's time to start marketing. Remember, we said earlier that marketing is just giving your client one great experience after another. Also, the third pillar of our "bottom line of business" is to inform, educate and convince our customers that we can meet their needs. Content Marketing is how we can bring all of this together.

It's Cold Outside

How you present your content is based mainly on where the prospective client is in relationship to your business. In marketing, we often refer to this as "traffic" and it is often determined by the "temperature" of the relationship. We will characterize this as cold, warm and hot.

Cold Traffic refers to those who have never seen your company before or have never engaged with you in a meaningful way. These people need an introduction to you or your brand. From our dating scenario, these are people that you are meeting for the very first time.

Warm Traffic are those who are familiar with you. They have engaged in some of your content, they have attended a webinar or downloaded your free gift. But, they have never purchased from you. In our scenario, these are people that you have exchanged text messages with, called on the phone or even met for coffee or lunch. You are friendly but you are not in a committed relationship.

Hot Traffic are people that have bought from you before. They may have purchased a $7 tripwire or a $499 coaching program. These are people that are in relationship with you. It's important that you continue to "date" these clients. I know I have said it before but it is worth repeating. Many times, the answer to increasing the revenue in our business is not finding more clients but finding ways to help the clients we already have at a higher level.

The Almighty Blog

One of the easiest and most effective marketing strategies you can use in your business is blogging. Blogging allows you to publish relevant content about your industry while increasing the exposure of you and your brand to your target market. Blogging, when done right, can help you build your list, engage with your audience and increase your company's sales. Here are a few reasons why you need to take your business' blog seriously.

Blogging allows you to create content that will attract your target audience.

While we often credit Google for providing information about anything you can think of, the truth is, Google provides very little of the content that we find on web. Google is just a search engine. What is it searching? It is searching all the content that has been published on the internet by people like you and me. When you search "how to build a landing page," Google goes to its handy dandy index and gives you a list of all the pages on the web that talk about 'building a landing page." Those pages, many of them blog posts, were written by people just like us, who have something to say about building landing pages. When you click on a particular post, you are taken AWAY from Google and TO the website that the content is found on. From there, you can read the article or click around to see if there is other information on the site that you are interested in.

Blogging allows your content to be searchable

Let's say that you wrote a great Facebook post on how to build a landing page. Guess what? The person we mentioned above that is searching on Google for that topic will never find your post. Why? Because content that you post on Facebook is NOT searchable on Google. Most content that is posted on social media is NOT searchable through search engines. For your content to be searchable, it must be on your website or a third-party platform such as YouTube which is searchable by Google (especially since YouTube is owned by Google).

Blogging allows you to showcase your expertise

Your blog content allows you to showcase your knowledge and expertise. Readers will have a chance to experience how you are able to help them solve their problem. When you can produce several targeted pieces of content on a given area, it increases your credibility.

However, blogging is not just about writing a bunch of content and posting it on your website. Blogging is a main source of ungated content and therefore an important part of your sales process. Blogs are sometimes the first introduction that someone has to you or your products and services.

Below are a few mistakes to avoid when producing your blog.

Mistake #1 – Not using your blog for list building

Your blog should be the number 1 vehicle you use for list building. Why? Because it allows you to engage with your audience after they have left your site. Having lots of visitors each day on your site is great but if you are not able to engage with them through email marketing afterwards, you are leaving money on the table. Also, you are leaving people without the help they may need from some of your other products and services. Make sure that you include some type of lead magnet or freemium on each blog post with an opt-in form.

Mistake #2 – You are not utilizing the power of retargeting

Every one that leaves your blog, or website for that fact, should leave with a little "gift," or a little pixel. Retargeting pixels, especially for Facebook advertising is easy to install and will allow you to run specific ads to those people who are already familiar with you and have already visited your site. You can better segment your target audience for advertising. For instance, if I have visited your site and read your blog post on "Ways to Remove Gluten from Your Diet," I am probably more likely to buy your book on

Gluten Free Cooking than I am to buy your book on Low Carb Meals.

Mistake #3 – Not having a plan in place for where you want this relationship to go

Your blog is often the beginning point of your relationship with a potential reader. Where do you want this relationship to go? Thinking, "I just want them to buy something," is not good enough. You want them to buy what? What is it going to take for them to feel ready to commit to that type of purchase? Are there smaller purchases available that they should make first? Remember, you are developing a relationship with each person that reads your content. You must take the lead and determine where you are going.

Types of Blog Posts

One of a blogger's biggest challenge is coming up with great blog posts that will be interesting to their readers. Not only is content important, but the way that content is presented is also key. Below are a few types of blog posts you may want to include on your site to add a little kick to your blog.

The Embed Reactor

This is a method that I learned from Ryan Deiss of Digital Marketer. You find a popular YouTube video on your subject matter (one with over a million views). You embed the YouTube video into your post and you write a short "reaction" to it. You may agree or disagree with the content. It's up to you. Make sure that you mention who it is in the video and link back to their site.

The Quote Post

You can compile a list of quotes about a particular topic. For instance, you can pull together "The Best Marketing Advice from Top Women CEOs." Of course, make sure to accurately quote the statement and who first said it. If you add a "Tweet This" button, you will probably get even more interaction.

The Round Up List Post

These posts are extremely popular because people love lists. The great thing about these posts is that you can curate content from others, as long as you link back to the source. For instance, you can make a list of "The Top 10 Business Coaches You Should Follow This Year." Don't forget to put yourself on the list.

Infographics

Infographics are great to add to a blog post. Many times, infographics will include source code that you can easily embed into your site that will show the graphics and properly credit the source. Make sure that you add a pin on Pinterest for your post because Pinterest readers love infographics.

Content Marketing is a great way to inform, educate and convince your customers that you can meet their needs. However, having great content is not enough. You must drive traffic to that content and get people to see it.

Chapter 5 - Your Paid Traffic

Having products and services, along with well thought out content to promote them, is great but you must make sure that someone sees all this great stuff you offer. People cannot respond to your offer if they don't see it.

Unfortunately, just because there are millions of people surfing the internet and hanging out on social media, it doesn't mean that they are looking at your website or engaging with your social media posts. You must drive traffic to your content.

Traffic comes in two forms, paid and unpaid. In a perfect world, you would put your great offer out there on the internet and people who have the problem that your product solves would flock to your site to evaluate your offer. Well, it just doesn't happen that way. The line, "Build it and they will come," was great in the movie "Field of Dreams" but not in real life. You must go get your traffic, at least to begin with.

Unpaid traffic, also known as "organic" traffic, happens when someone comes to your site without you paying for it. Maybe they searched something on Google and your page came up in the search results and they clicked the link to arrive at your site. They may follow you on social media and saw a post or someone may have told them about your site.

Organic traffic is great; however, it is not always plentiful. You must do a lot of work to get your website to the point where it will receive a lot of traffic organically. While there are some Search Engine Optimization (SEO) things you can do, the complicated algorithms that Google and other search engines use make it virtually impossible to count on organic traffic to get in front of the right people. This makes it difficult when you are first starting out. That is why you must include a paid traffic strategy in your digital marketing plan.

Paid Ads

I believe that paid ads are the best way to get targeted traffic to your offers, especially when you are first starting out. However, you must have a strategy that accounts for the relationship based business methodology that we discussed in the introduction. This is where I believe many small business owners make their mistake when it comes to using paid ads. You still must make sure that you are making the correct offer to the right people based on where you are in relationship to them.

Targeting the Right Audience

Figuring out the right audience for a given ad can be one of the most complicated parts of the ad process. Therefore, it is so important that you figure out your customer avatar. It's not important to just know what problems your target market has and what keeps them up at night. You need to know where these people hangout, especially in cyberspace. What sites do they visit? What social media platforms are they on and who are they following on those platforms? If you get this wrong, and you will from time to time, you will find that your ads are not effective.

So, what do you do? You make your best guess, based on your customer avatar, and tweak it as necessary. See what works and look at what doesn't work. Do your research and don't be afraid to try.

Relationship Based Ads

Make sure that you are making the appropriate offers, based on where you are in relationship to your audience. An "offer" is not just a paid program. An offer may be an invitation to get a lead magnet or even to read a blog post. Your offers can't just be about getting the sale. They must cover relationship building and engagement as well.

If you are running ads to a target audience that is not familiar with you, you may want to run that ad to your ungated information. **Yes, run an ad to free information that doesn't even ask for an email address.** Why? Many of these people are "cold traffic" to you. They have never heard of you. Your offer is basically an introduction. You are saying, "Hi, I'm Vanessa. You have a problem that I can solve. Can we spend a few minutes together?" That's it. You are not asking for money or even an email address. You are just asking for a few moments of their time.

Once they come to your site (once they are in your house) things change. You can, and should, make an offer to move the relationship to the next level after they have consumed your free content. Therefore, your blog posts should have a call to action for your lead magnet, which will collect their information. You should have a sidebar on your blog that gives information about your tripwire offer and even your core offer. But more than anything else, you should have your site set up so that you can follow them around the web and remind them of the offer that they have seen and didn't accept. Remember, it can take 7 to 12 times for someone to see your offer before they decide to act. You must stay in front of that audience.

Retargeting

It's happened to you before. You went on a site, like Amazon or Best Buy and looked at something, maybe a new laptop. You spent a few moments on the site and then decided to do something else. Later that day, you were on Facebook and to your surprise, an ad shows up on Facebook for the EXACT item you were looking at before on Amazon. The next day, you go to Yahoo and BAM, there it is again. You notice for the next several days these ads appear to follow you on social media.

Welcome to the world of retargeting. Retargeting is a technology based method that allows your offer to follow people who have been on your site. It is extremely effective because, in general, people need to see your offer between 7 – 12 times. Studies have shown that only 2% of web traffic will convert on the first visit. Retargeting allows you to digitally "follow up" with people who have been on your site.

Retargeting uses a simple JavaScript code. You place a pixel, a small piece of code, on your website. It's that simple. The pixel can't be seen and will not affect your site's performance. When someone new visits your site, the code drops a cookie in their browser. When you run ads targeting those that have this cookie, your ad will be shown to those people. This is a powerful tool that can increase your conversion rates tenfold.

Where Should You Be

One of the questions most asked is, "What social media platforms should I advertise on?" The answer is simple, the ones where your target market is. However, with that said, I think you should venture out a little into other platforms sometimes. Why? Because you never know exactly where people hangout. So, don't be afraid to spend a few dollars trying out new platforms. Don't spend your entire ad budget there but you may want to shake things up from time to time.

Chapter 6 - Your Social Media Presence

"We don't have a choice on whether we do social media, the question is how well we do it."

Erik Qualman

It is an undeniable fact; social media has changed the way we do business. From Facebook statuses, Twitter tweets to YouTube video post, there has been a major shift in how information is communicated and consumed. Twenty-five years ago, people got their news by watching newscast that came on only during certain times of the day. Fifteen years ago, people got their news from their home log in screens such as Yahoo or America Online (AOL). Now, the news finds them on Facebook, Twitter or Livestream such as Periscope.

The Social Success Cycle

How do you get social media to work for you? To be most successful on social media, you need to have a strategy in place. The strategy that I have found to be the most successful is known as the "Social Success Cycle." I don't know the origin of the term but I was first introduced to it by Ryan Deiss and Russ Henneberry from Digital Marketer when I was studying for my Social and Community Manager certification. I found the concept to be fascinating because there were parts of it that I was already doing and found it to be rewarding. On the other hand, there were parts that I wasn't doing and that explained why I wasn't having success in those areas.

The Social Success Cycle consists of four parts.

- Social Listening
- Social Influencing
- Social Networking
- Social Selling

Notice that social selling is the LAST step in the cycle. This is where a lot of people mess up. They start out trying to sell without listening, influencing or networking. You must date your audience.

Social Listening

It is my personal belief that social listening is the most important piece of the puzzle. If you are not listening, you are not able to respond properly. Think about this. If you put your fingers in your ears and closed your eyes and then tried to have a conversation with me, it would be a hot mess. You wouldn't be responding to what I was saying. You would be talking about what you wanted to talk about. If I then started talking about what you were talking about and asked you questions about it, you couldn't respond because you couldn't hear me. That is what it looks like when you post a bunch of stuff on Facebook, Twitter, Periscope, or LinkedIn and you haven't listened to your marketplace.

Social Listening is monitoring and responding to customer service and reputation management issues on social networks. It also includes listening and observing your target audience and finding out what issues they have that you can solve. Some people live their lives on social media. They post every thought they have. Does that irritate you? Does it get on your nerves? STOP IT! Never, ever say that again, particularly if you are a coach. I love to see people post about their problems with technology. Why? That means I don't have to guess what problems they are having, they are telling me.

That is why you need to be in groups that your target market is in. If you are an author, being in a group with other authors will not help you in terms of sales. You need to be in the groups with people who would read your book.

This isn't just limited to social media. You should be listening wherever you are. If you are in an online class, listen to what people are talking about. Listen to their questions and concerns. Do they have problems that your company can provide a solution for?

I was recently part of a coaching class and was inspired to develop a service offering based on problems that students where having in the class. Dawniel Winningham teaches a fantastic course, LiveStream University, which shows you how to use platforms such as Periscope and Facebook Live, to promote your business. If you have ever seen her on livestream, you know that she is a beast when it comes to marketing on that platform. Well, she is also a beast when it comes to students in her class not having their homework.

The assignment involved the students doing their livestream on Periscope or Facebook Live daily. Well, that doesn't seem so hard, right? However, Dawniel has one rule of thumb, you don't go live without an offer. It can be an offer for a free report or it can be to your core offer. It didn't matter. You needed to have a call to action that drove people to your landing page.

Well, that was the issue. Many people in the class did not have a landing page. They didn't have a website. They had products and services but they had no way of completing those transactions (remember the "bottom line of business?") These people needed landing pages.

I wish I could say that I was "listening" and responded appropriately on my own. I didn't. While I was accustomed to "social listening" while scrolling down my Facebook feed or checking out LinkedIn groups, I totally missed this opportunity, initially. It took Dawniel, who is also my business coach, to literally say to me, "Vanessa, why don't you offer to do landing pages." After her telling me that a few times, I "listened." (Hey, let me know if you need a landing page or two.)

Tips for Social Listening

Find 3 Facebook groups and 3 LinkedIn groups where the audience is that have the problems that you solve and join them. Spend 5 minutes a day monitoring those groups. Get a notebook and jot down notes about what people are struggling with. Also, don't forget to listen in other online gatherings such as classes or webinars.

Social Influencing

To have a successful human dating relationship, you must show that you have something to bring to the table. You must show that you are a giving person. This is the phase of the relationship where you try to be as helpful as possible. Instead of going out to eat, you decide to cook a romantic dinner. For the gentleman, this maybe where you offer to fix the leaky faucet because you want to show that you are helpful around the house.

Social Influencing on the web is very similar. It involves establishing authority on social networks through the distribution and sharing of valuable content. This is where you need your content marketing. You can dazzle your audience with your brilliance by creating valuable content. This is where you show that you have your finger on the pulse of your niche or industry because you are sharing the content of others that are respected in your field. You show them that you are an expert. This is where the action and hard work come in.

In my opinion, this is the most important part of the cycle. Yes, I know I said that about social listening. But if you just listen and never act, never create content and distribute it, never get on Periscope, never write your blog post, never do a Facebook Live... if you never do anything with that information that you heard, you are just a stalker. STOP IT. Take that information you jotted down during the social listening exercise and now develop some products and services. Do some Periscopes or write a blog post for the solution to a problem you heard. Share some information with your audience from someone else. Stop just "listening" and DO something.

Tips for Social Influencing

Find 3 real issues that your audience is having (use your social listening exercise). Develop a FREE digital product that solves a portion of that problem. You can write a blog post (if you don't have a blog, you can publish it on LinkedIn Pulse), do a series on Periscope or Facebook Live. You can record a video or and audio, it doesn't matter. Do something!

Social Networking

There are some powerful people that can help take your business to the next level but they don't know who you are. Likewise, there are some great influencers in your industry that you don't know. It's time to change that.

Social Networking involves finding and associating with authoritative and influential people and brands on social networks. This is key to building your brand and audience. You must get in front of more people. The best way to do that is to have people put you in front of their audience. The best way to accomplish this is to put these people in front of your audience.

In my opinion, this is the most important part of the cycle. Yes, I know I said that about social listening and social influencing. But, if you just listen and never act; or if you listen, act and create content but it never gets beyond your audience, your business will not grow. You must partner and collaborate with people to get your content in front of more people.

I have found that the best way to do this is by sharing other people's content with my audience. This has a ton of benefits. First, it allows me to share great content with my audience that I did not have to create. It allows me to share information about great upcoming events that my audience could be interested in. Listen, there is no room for competition. There is enough business to go around. When you show yourself friendly, you will be amazed at the business opportunities that become available.

This is how I landed one of my first "big" clients, Peak Performers Institute. The founders, Che Brown and Trevor Otts, are two of the greatest business minds of our time. I was asked to be a part of their team because of social networking, but I didn't know that was what I was doing at the time.

In February 2015, I had never heard of them. I received an email about an event that they were having called "72 Hours of Power." That virtual event was so life changing for my business mindset that I was hooked. I started attending their Google Hangouts and I participated in their virtual Facebook group. I started doing social networking but I didn't know what that was at the time. I was just following directions. Trevor would say, "In the group, post your first name, your last name, where you are from and a little bit about your business." I did it.

He would ask us to post the nuggets in the Facebook group that we got from the session we were listening to. I did that but, I took it one step further. I had taken Sandi Krakowski's Twitter class so I decide to open another browser and not only post those take-a-ways in the Facebook group, I decided to post them on Twitter where, in my mind, "other people would see it." Instead of putting the name of the person that had given the nugget, I would add their Twitter handle. It took a little extra work because I haven't heard of any of the people that were on the platform. So, I took the extra 30 seconds to look them up and grab their Twitter handles for the posts. It was worth it.

Guess what happen? When those speakers finished speaking, they would look at their Twitter account and I would have blown up their notifications with what they had said. They loved it because it promoted them as a speaker and showed that someone was listening. They would retweet it and would follow me. Well, when others saw that Mr. or Mrs. Big Shot was retweeting my tweets, they would start following me as well. I ended up on Twitter lists for social media experts and small business gurus because I was sharing awesome content, even though it wasn't mine. Eventually, I got a call from Trevor Otts and Che Brown commending me for my engagement and asking me to be on their team. Those shares resulted in thousands of dollars of business for my company.

Tips for Social Networking

Find the 5 to 10 influencers in your industry and begin engaging with them online. Read and comment on their blogs. Share their events in Facebook and Twitter and make sure to tag them, if possible.

Social Selling

Finally, we get to the point where we can successfully make offers. I am not saying to wait until you master the other 3 steps before you make offers. You need to be doing all of this at the same time. However, you may not see great success with your offers until the first 3 items are clearly in motion.

Also, you want to make sure that you make the right offer to the right person at the right time in your relationship. You need a variety of things in your online superstore. You need free offers for people that don't know you. This could be blog posts, videos or content rich social media posts. You need lead magnet offers that provide solutions to very specific problems in exchange for their email addresses so that you are building your email list. Followers on your social media sites are worth zero until they get on your list. You need low priced products that you can offer to those that want to try you out. You need mid-range and high end products as well.

In my opinion, this is the most important part of the cycle. Yes, I know I said that about social listening, social influencing and social networking. But if you just listen and never act; or if you listen, act and create content but it never gets beyond your audience; or you create content that goes viral but you don't make the offer, you won't sell anything and you won't make money. You can't pay your bills with likes and comments. You must convert your social media audience into buyers.

So, there it is, the Social Success Cycle. It starts with social listening, then social influencing, then social networking and finally social selling. But it doesn't end there. You must continue to listen, produce content, connect with influencers and make the sell.

Sound overwhelming. It doesn't have to be. Here is a 20 minute a day Social Success Cycle Power Plan that will turn you into a profitable, online social butterfly in no time.

Social Listening – Each day choose 1 Facebook or LinkedIn Group to monitor. Spend 5 minutes looking at the conversations and questions that were asked. Take notes.

Social Influencing – When you find a problem that was asked that you can solve, spend 5 minutes outlining a solution. Schedule a time that you will complete the solution (blog post, video, audio, etc.).

Social Networking – Use Twitter lists to organize key followers in your industry. Spend 5 minutes reviewing, responding and retweeting their comments.

Social Selling – Make sure that you are posting an offer at least one a day. However, your offer should not be more than 10-20% of the posts you make each day so make sure that you are posting other things as well.

Chapter 7 - Your Emails

Contrary to popular belief, email marketing is far from dead. Many smart entrepreneurs use email marketing because it works. Consider these facts as reported by Web Presence Solutions in January 2017.

- It is reported that for every dollar spent on email marketing, an average of **$44 dollar return on investment** is realized. (Source: Campaign Monitor, 2016)

- More than 86% of businesses surveyed indicate that they plan to increase their upcoming **email marketing budgets**. (Source: Email on Acid, 2016)

- The number of **e-mail users in the US** is projected to grow to 244.5 million by the end of 2017. That number is forecast to grow to 254.7 million by 2020. (Source: Statista, 2016)

While there may be other communication vehicles that are getting attention, such as text message marketing, email is still important. Since email marketing isn't going anywhere anytime soon, let's look at the 3 types of emails you need in your business.

Transactional

Transactional emails document the transactions that occur between you and your customers. It could be an email that provides a receipt for a purchase or an email that acknowledges that a class registration has been received. These emails are usually triggered in that something must happen (i.e. the purchase of an item) for the email to be sent.

Relational

These are emails that you send to engage with your audience and provide valuable content. This may be in the form of a newsletter or an email that is part of an automation campaign. These emails are usually sent in between promotional email campaigns.

Promotional

Promotional emails let your list know about products and services that you are offering. For many business owners, it seems as if these are the only emails they know how to send; the ones that say, "Buy my stuff."

Email Automation

Having a solid email marketing strategy is more than just having emails set up to be sent out on a schedule. Emails should be triggered not just by time, but by behavior. Your email marketing system should be able to send emails based on what your audience does or doesn't do.

A simple, timed based email strategy may look something like this:

- Immediately – Email sent when person signs up for lead magnet. (Transactional email)

- Day 1 – Follow up to lead magnet, offer additional valuable content. (Relational email)

- Day 3 – Email with additional content, maybe from a blog post. (Relational email)

- Day 5 – Email with more content and an offer to purchase the tripwire offer. (Promotional email)

- Day 7 - Email with more content (Relational email)

- Day 9 – Email with more content (Relational email)

- Day 11 – Email offering core offer (Promotional email)

If you don't have any email strategy in place, the above schedule is a good place to start. However, it is far from what a real, automated strategy looks like. A real automated strategy looks at the behavior of the people receiving the email and the next email is based on that behavior.

It may look something like this:

- Immediately – Email sent when person signs up for lead magnet. (Transactional email)

  o If email is opened and the link clicked, the person would proceed to the next email on the scheduled date.

  o If the email is opened but the link is not clicked, the person would get an email reminding them to click the link to download the lead magnet.

- If the email is not opened, the person is sent this email again perhaps with a different subject line.

- Day 1 – Follow up to lead magnet, offer additional valuable content. (Relational email)

  - If email is opened, the person would proceed to the next email on the scheduled date.

  - If the email is not opened, the person is sent this email again perhaps with a different subject line.

- Day 3 – Email with additional content, maybe from a blog post. (Relational email)

  - If email is opened, the person would proceed to the next email on the scheduled date.

  - If the email is not opened, the person is sent this email again perhaps with a different subject line.

- Day 5 – Email with more content and an offer to purchase the tripwire offer. (Promotional email)

- If email is opened and the link clicked, the person would proceed to the next email on the scheduled date.

- If the email is opened but the link is not clicked, the person would get an email reminding them to click the link to download the lead magnet.

- If the email is not opened, the person is sent this email again perhaps with a different subject line.

- Day 7 - Email with more content (Relational email)

  - If email is opened, the person would proceed to the next email on the scheduled date.

  - If the email is not opened, the person is sent this email again perhaps with a different subject line.

- Day 9 – Email with more content (Relational email)

  - If email is opened, the person would proceed to the next email on the scheduled date.

- ○ If the email is not opened, the person is sent this email again perhaps with a different subject line.

- Day 11 – Email offering core offer (Promotional email)

  - ○ If email is opened, the person would proceed to the next email on the scheduled date.

  - ○ If the email is not opened, the person is sent this email again perhaps with a different subject line.

Most good email marketing solutions like GetResponse, Aweber and Constant Contact can handle this type of automation. It takes time to set something like this up but it is worth it.

Segmentation

Email marketing is also a good way to segment your list. One way to use this strategy is to see what other products and services you offer that your audience may be interested in. Once you know what they are interested in, you can start engaging with them about that product solution.

An easy way to do this is to send an email to your list offering them a new lead magnet. The purpose of this is not to get their email (you already have that) but to see what other items they are interested in.

For instance, you may be a health and wellness coach. You have built your list based on content that deal specifically with nutrition and exercise. You are thinking about expanding your subject matter to cover weight loss. You would develop a lead magnet that you would not only use to grow your list but to also see who you current have on your list that is interested in that subject. If your email marketing platform supports it, you could "tag" these people so that you market to them easily. Your initial email sequence may look something like this:

Email to the entire list offering them the new lead magnet. It includes a link to a landing page with an opt in form.

- If email is opened, link clicked and form filled out, the person would be sent the transactional email that delivered the lead magnet and "tagged" in the system as a person that is highly interested.

- If the email is opened, link clicked but form not filled out, the person would get an email reminding them to complete the form to get the free gift. The person is tagged as "interested."

- If the email is opened but the link is not clicked, the person is sent another email maybe worded differently.

- If the email is not opened, the person is sent this email again perhaps with a different subject line or the person isn't sent anything at all because they are not interested in the subject matter.

Chapter 8 – Conclusion

Congratulations! If you have made it this far, you are well on your way to mastering these 5 key components in your business.

- Your Sales Funnel
- Your Content
- Your Paid Traffic
- Your Social Media
- Your Email Marketing

But the party is JUST STARTING. I appreciate you purchasing this book. I love that you may have left a review on Amazon (please do it you haven't) or you have reached out to me at Vanessa@DigitalMasteryForWomen.com).

But, my goal is not to just give you great information. My goal is to help you implement some of the great ideas you got while reading this book.

Next Steps

If you are new to business or digital marketing, your head may be spinning right now from all the information and ideas that are colliding in your brain. That's a good thing. However, we must organize some of this stuff so that you can move forward. My first assignment for you is to go to the Online Resource Hub and download the "What's Missing" checklist and inventory what is missing in your digital marketing strategy. This will give you an idea of what resources you need to move forward with developing your digital marketing strategy.

www.VanessaCollinsLLC.com/DMFWBook

I hope that you have found this book to be helpful. Please reach out to me if I can assist you with your digital marketing strategy.

Other Books by Heart Thoughts Publishing

Intensive Faith Therapy – Vanessa Collins
The Promises of Jesus – Vanessa Collins
The Promises of God – Vanessa Collins
50 Mistakes Grant Writers Make – Vanessa Collins
Transcending Greatness – Lawrence Perkins
Lil Fella's Big Dream – Lawrence Perkins
Lupe and Kita – Lawrence Perkins
One Way – Dorsey Howard
The Start of a Healing Conversation – Edgar Gosa
Breakfast with God – Paul Jakes, Jr.
Pace Learns a Lesson – Cynthia Wilson
Every Day A Winner - By Aaron Gilbert
There's an Elephant in the Room – Cynthia Wilson
The Problem with Jesus – Aretha Tatum
Becky's Kidneys – Paulette Miles
From the Jewelry Box - Sheila Spencer
Moving From Religion To Relationship - Neisha-Ann
Thompson
TJ and Randy's Big Weekend – Lawrence Perkins
Flatline Your Ego Mind - James Page
Jasmine's Big Secret - Lawrence Perkins
Fifty Shades of Faith – Stephanie Flores
Three Generations Cooking With Sole - Pamela Ward
Karissa's Amazing Invitation To Visit The Queen - Sharon
Nelson
The Alphabets: El Alfabeto - Ari Armour
The Wonderful Counselor – Aretha Tatum
Some Good Things to Consider on the Way to See God -
Derrick Collins
Finn The Freckled Fish – Antionette Reese
Enough: Say "NO" to Dieting - JoAnn Turner
Stayin' Alive Ain't No Jive - Charles Vance

Visit us at www.HeartThoughtsPublishing.com
Or email us at
Info@HeartThoughtsPublishing.com